A Silly Book

(stories & common sense)

Joseph Hart

Contents

STORIES

"Science is the history of dead religions."

- Oscar Wilde

"He makes a virtue of his tastes."

- Charles Dickens

The House Of God

The man knelt worshiping God in fervent prayer. God came upon him and was curious at such devotion. He touched the man on the forehead so that the man could tell only the truth. And God said, "Why do you love me?"

And the man answered, "I don't. I despise you. You are cruel and dishonest. You are unkind and unfair. I gave more love in my short life than you have given throughout all eternity. I hate you."

And God said, "Then why do you worship me?"

And the man answered, "Because I'm afraid I'll go to hell if I don't."

And God said, "Then you do believe in me. That is enough."

And the man said, "Yes, I believe in you. But I didn't want to. I wanted to be an Atheist."

And there was silence in the House of God.

And God came upon a woman who was weeping with love of him. Her face was beautiful with joy. And God touched her on the forehead so that she could tell only the truth. And God said, "Why do you love me?"

And the woman answered, "Because I hated my neighbor and you gave her a stillborn child. Because you had me born into power and wealth. Because you have sent my enemies to burn forever in hell. These are things that I would have done. That is why I love you."

And there was silence in the House of God.

Then God came upon a man who was lacerating himself with thorns, while kneeling at an altar. He was bleeding, but his face was ecstatic.

And God touched him on the forehead so that he could tell only the truth. And God said, "Why do you love me?"

And the man answered, "I was born homosexual. My family hated me when I was a child. As I grew up, the villagers hated me. They hated me because I'm homosexual. Through them I learned to hate myself. Then I found that you hate me too. That is why I love you."

And there was silence in the House of God.

11-4-84

Truth

He had been unconscious for seven hours. Then his heart stopped beating. He was dead.

But they employed desperate measures. They roused him.

As he awoke, his first sound was, "Ppfgugh?"

They noted his first sound and showed it to him. Had he brought back a truth from death?

But what he had said was incomprehensible. And worse, it was a question. He couldn't remember.

Debunked

"You're heartless," she said weeping sullenly into her blue hankie. "You've taken away the only thing that gave me comfort, solace, purpose."

"I'm sorry, mother," he said. "I had to explain away your God. It was making me unhappy."

The Tradition Of Clocks

At birth each child was ceremonially given a clock. It was wound and set. He would keep this clock for the rest of his life, which was brief. When the alarm in his clock rang, the person died. It had been this way for generations.

Then he was born. He was given his clock. However, when he was old enough to understand the purpose of the clock, he said, "How silly!" And he broke his clock.

The others were horrified and outraged. However, he lived a very long time. Much longer than anyone had ever lived.

1969

Acrophobia

He had a withering horror of heights. They terrified him. He went to a psychiatrist, and after several months of hard work, his fear went away. He was free. He was happy. He climbed to the top of the Statue of Liberty and jumped off.

The Bouquet Of Flowers

He loved her, but he was afraid to tell her. He felt unworthy.

Then she went to the hospital for a minor operation, and he wanted to take her a bouquet of flowers. He went to the florist and bought it. But he was afraid she wouldn't want flowers from him. He was afraid they would anger and disgust her. So he threw the flowers away. He was very confused and unhappy.

He saw her again after she had left the hospital. He smiled and asked after her. And she said, "What do you care? You didn't come to visit me even one time." And she walked away.

The Atheist

She loved her television preacher. Her husband was an Atheist. He tolerated the money she sent to the preacher's television show. The preacher ended each show with, "I love you. As Jesus loves you, so do I."

Then it caved in. He was convicted of taking money from his audience for his own use.

Her husband said nothing. But she approached him with rage, crying, "You delight in this, don't you! But you will burn in hell for this! You are a heathen! He loved me! He loved me! He loved me!"

David And The Man On The Streetcar

It happened in the fall of 1966. He was in San Francisco. He was riding in a crowded streetcar. Bodies were pressed against bodies. And the contact, unless indifferent, was pleasant. Then he felt the rhythmic movement of a body against his own. He felt and heard breathing in his ear. Someone was masturbating against him. Then the car stopped. The man behind him moved quickly out. He looked hurried and embarrassed.

Then he saw David. He loved him before he knew his name. David was pretty. He had a flat, negroid nose and long brown hair that he parted in the middle. He wanted to embrace him, to hold him, to kiss him, to become him. But he didn't.

The Saint

During his childhood, he had all desire beaten out of him. He wanted nothing.

When he was twenty years old, he entered a monastery. He followed all the rules. They told him what to do. He was happy.

Thirty years later, someone asked him whether he believed in God. He said, "Of course not. Why should I?"

He was told to leave the monastery.

He moved to NYC where jobs were easy to get. He found work washing dishes in a restaurant. He did this for twenty years. Then he died. No one either knew or cared that he was dead. He just didn't come to work.

Belief

His friends were sitting in his living room, and he was pacing the floor in front of them. He was enraged. He cried, "Everything is phony! Nothing is real! You claim to be my friends. I don't believe you exist!" His friends vanished. "This room," he yelled, "is artificial. Chairs don't exist in nature. This manufactured box that I live in is unreal. It doesn't exist. I don't believe that it exists!"

The house vanished and he was standing on an open space of ground. In front of him stood a full-length mirror. He looked at it, and his image said, "Do you believe that I exist?"

1968

Lost

He left home for work at 8 o'clock as he had done every morning for the past twenty-two years. He passed things so familiar that he hardly noticed them. Then he passed some unfamiliar things. But it didn't bother him. Soon he was passing more unfamiliar things than familiar ones. Then he was passing no familiar things at all. He circled back and turned corners almost randomly. But it didn't help. He was lost.

Finally he saw a phone booth. He parked beside it and went into it. He dialed his home. There were several rings, then a voice said, "I'm sorry. You have reached a number that has been disconnected or is no longer in use. If you feel you have reached this recording in error, please check your directory and try again. Thank you."

1972

The Beast

He ran through the streets shouting that the beast was coming. The beast was near. Like Cassandra, he was ignored. Panting, he stopped by a shop and looked at his reflection in the window. He saw the massive brow, the tangled hair, the yellow fangs.

Paradox

She was an Atheist. She was a concert violinist with a wonderful career. Then she was blinded in an auto accident.

She became depressed and passive. She stopped caring about anything. Her mother came and lived with her.

Her mother was a rabid Christian who for years had unsuccessfully proselytized her daughter. This was her chance.

The mother called the parson who came. She left   him and her daughter together. The preacher droned on with his monotonous drivel. Finally the girl felt a stirring inside her. The feeling increased. At last this crescendo of emotion exploded with volcanic force. She stood and shouted, "Oh, get out of here, you damned fool!" And her eyesight returned.

The Wound

He was playing at home in the back yard. He fell and skinned his elbow. It bled. Crying, he went to show his mother.

He held his elbow up for her to see, and she said, "It'll heal. Get out of here. I'm busy."

He returned to the back yard and resumed playing.

Overnight a scab formed on the wound.

The next day at school, he fell again and knocked the scab off. It hurt. A teacher saw this and came to comfort him. And he was afraid.

Teleology

He was three months old, and the ancient hag held him in her arms. He liked the smell of her, and relaxed in her embrace. He liked the intricate colored earring that dangled from her left ear. It fascinated him.

Then the old woman bent her head close to the baby's ear and whispered, "All religions are bogus."

When he was older, understanding was retroactive. The words were lodged deep in his mind. Never in his life did he feel any curiosity about religion. Any religion.

Werther

Jim loved Ted. Ted loved Kathy. Kathy wanted Jim. Ted and Kathy were married. Ted was tall, angular, gaunt and blond. Kathy was large and dark.

Kathy told Jim she would kill herself unless he fucked her. He refused. Ted came home and found her dying on the living room floor. She was saved.

So Jim fucked Kathy.

Kathy told Ted she would divorce him unless Jim continued to fuck her. Ted consented.

Jim finally left. They had been like ghosts to him. And when he was gone, it was as though he had never been there at all.

1965

Her

He loved her. Deeply. And lightly. Each little thing she did delighted him.

He was afraid of her. But he wanted to profess his love. So he did.

And she rebuffed him.

And he was relieved.

1985

Deja Vu

"He sat down in the restaurant and perused the menu. Then the waitress came to his table and said – What would you like to order, Mr. Brown? He asked – How did you know my name? She replied – The man at the small table told me. He turned and looked. There was no one sitting at the small table."

Having written this much, he put down his pen and relaxed.

The waitress, seeing that he was no longer writing, came to his table. She asked, "Would you like to order something now, Mr. Green?" He asked, "How do you know my name?" She answered, "The man at the small table told me." He turned and looked. There was no one sitting at the small table.

John's Corner

He hated John.

So he bought some bricks, some cement, some chalk, a large silver key, and a sandwich.

He went to a distant dark corner in his cellar. It was lighted by a single uncovered bulb dangling from the ceiling. With the chalk he drew the picture of a door on one of the walls. He put the key on the floor, near the picture of a door. He put the sandwich bedside the key. He piled the bricks in the corner. He mixed the cement and left it near the bricks.

Then he went upstairs, phoned John and pleasantly asked him over.

In his living room, ostensibly as a game, he hypnotized John. Then he took him downstairs and stood him in the corner. He told John to brick himself into the corner and then, using the large silver key, to unlock the door on the wall and come back up to the living room. He also told him to eat the sandwich when he was hungry.

Then he sat and watched John wall himself into the corner. When the last brick was in place, he stood up, switched off the light and left.

1966

A Farewell To Hemingway

"Is this not a fine balcony?" she said.

"Yes," I said. "It's fine, darling. Isn't it?"

"Yes, it's lovely, darling."

"And fine," I said.

"Yes, darling. And fine. Isn't that a fine sea below us?"

"Yes, darling. It's homicidal, you know."

"Well, isn't that fine."

"It's no respecter of life. Isn't that lovely?"

"Yes, darling. It's just like us. Isn't that fine?"

"It's just fine. And look at those great big rocks."

"I know, darling. I can see them. They're just fine."

"If I tossed you off this balcony and you landed on your head on one of those great big rocks, your head would be smashed."

"Well, isn't that fine, darling?" she said.

"Yes, darling. There would be nothing left of your head but broken bone and blood and brain. Isn't that lovely?" I said.

"Yes, darling," she said. "It's just fine."

1993

Epigrams

Everyone is justifiable. No one is just.

Thinking is more interesting than believing.

One sees god in a beautiful sunrise. What does one see in a head cold?

An autobiography is how one sees oneself. What one actually is, is a matter for science.

Many things make sense. Not all of them are true.

It is often difficult to distinguish between what makes sense and what one is merely used to.

It isn't that I disbelieve Christianity, it's that I dislike it.

If there were no heaven, there would be no god.

It's blasphemous to believe in god. It means he has no conscience.

Without reason, one would be lost. Yet, there is no reason.

If religions didn't feel good, there would be no religions.

God is impossible.

1997

COMMON SENSE

Someone asked Isaac Asimov whether he believed in God.

He answered, "Whose?"

The church that collapses on Sunday, killing or injuring the faithful in the act of devotion -

The mother who thanks god for bringing her son safely back from war, the war in which other mothers' sons were injured or killed -

How is the soul of a person superior to that of a plant?

In the Christian hereafter, god is an electrode giving eternal pleasure to countless lumps of disincarnate believers.

What friend could love the god that sent his friend to hell?

God cannot be disproved, neither can leprechauns.

I am to believe the Bible solely because the Bible tells me to.

What is the virtue of belief, the wickedness of disbelief?

One man's god is another man's nonsense.

If god is love, he doesn't exist.

It's as easy to imagine an eternal universe as an eternal god.

No compassionate person can be a Christian.

If Christianity were true, it couldn't be disproved.

Without pleasure, nothing is good. Without pain, nothing is bad.

God, not the devil, hates the truth.

God loves the belief, not the believer.

Hell refutes a god of love.

Disbelief destroys god.

Religion is a game.

Omnipotence is impossible because some actions are mutually exclusive.

Knowledge obviates faith.

What is the virtue of a virgin birth?

Thought is more interesting than belief.

If I encountered god, it would merely be an experience.

God enjoins pretense.

I am to believe that god created the entire universe solely to reward those members of one species on one planet who believe that god create the entire universe solely to reward them.

If there were no heaven, there would be no Christians.

Christianity has secondary gains.

Christians permit each other nothing, but allow god anything.

One is saved by believing that one is saved.

God created hell so he could save people from it.

If heaven is to be an eternity of mindless pleasure, what's wrong with sex?

By requiring me to believe the Bible, I am forced to read it.

What if I don't like god when I meet him?

Why don't rocks have souls?

The Bible is self-defining, not self-evident.

Many books claim to gave been inspired by god. How can I choose among them?

God is not fair, much less loving.

I prefer ghosts and seances to god.

When moralists talk about values, they just mean sex.

Religion is a delusion confirmed by others with the same delusion.

A person who does what god does is hung.

I have never felt loved by god.

God forgives everything except disbelief. Disbelief hurts no one.

I could not enjoy heaven knowing others were in hell.

Children believe what they are taught.

The final proof of the existence of god is the harm a believer can do to a nonbeliever.

Christian love is a duty.

God commands people to care for the needy. Yet god created the need and can do more to relieve it than people can.

People go to hell for telling the truth.

Revenge is not an endless thing.

Christianity is unnecessary without hell.

Christianity is imposed on experience, not derived from it.

Doctrines that dictate what one should feel are absurd. Like psychiatry.

If god exists, is that a reason to worship him?

It is impossible to love god. Except mindlessly.

If I were a Christian, I would be very unhappy. And I would dislike all my fellow Christians.

Christianity is a generality that discounts reasons and differences in people.

What does god think of birth defects?

The church opposes Darwin. It once opposed Galileo.

Something causes one to believe. That cause is not a good reason to believe.

Whether god exists is a matter of fact. There is nothing moral about it.

One must believe for the sake of it. One could be required to believe anything.

What is bad about sex?

Dead babies do not believe in god.

There is something wrong with a religion that must be taught to be known, written down to be remembered, explained to be understood.

There is no such thing as a victimless crime.

Religion ignores evidence and opposes inquiry.

Pornography is a harmless pleasure.

You can thank god for the miracle of modern medicine, but you still have to pay your doctor.

Prostitutes are paid to give pleasure. So are maiden piano teachers.

An artist desires to create something. But he doesn't know what will satisfy that desire until after he creates it.

Senility affects some old people. What is the good of a mindless soul?

The more one loves America, the less one loves freedom.

People kill for the religion they were taught, die for the country they were born in.

God created man in his own image. Which man?

If a person accepts one unfounded religion, he has no reason to reject any other.

Is it blasphemous to have sexual fantasies about Jesus?

Jesus preferred children. Children are born without belief. At what age did he prefer them?

If god exists, I'm willing to believe it. What more can I offer?

If one doubts the answer to an arithmetic problem, one is merely mistaken. If one doubts the existence of god, one goes to hell. Arithmetic is better.

When a Christian gives the reasons for his belief, he is considered holy. When a non-Christian gives his reasons for disbelief, he is burned at the stake.

If I were god, I would make plants insensate, all animals vegetarian and bigotry emotionally impossible.

If god makes sense, he doesn't exist. If he exists, he doesn't make sense.

Ethics have always been situational. The Bible says, "Thou shalt not kill," not "Thou shalt not kill people unless...".

Faith is believing what one knows to be false.

March 3, 1985

www.ingramcontent.com/pod-product-compliance
Lightning Source LLC
Chambersburg PA
CBHW030417160726
47992CB00007B/3169